Connecting

Also by Brenda Eldridge and published by Ginninderra Press

Poetry

The Silver Cord
It's All Good
A Personal View
Facing Cancer
From My Garden
Best Heard & Seen
Scarves
Tangled Roots: new & selected poems
Wonderment
Elemental (Pocket Poets)
Forgotten Dreams (Pocket Poets)
Big Blue Marble (Pocket Poets)
Silver Tree (Pocket Poets)
Coming of Age (Pocket Poets)
Fly Me Away (Pocket Poets)
Not What They Might Seem (Picaro Poets)

Non-fiction

Down by the River
Tales From My Patagonia
It's Still Out There
There's a Rainbow Serpent In My Garden
Eastwards
From Patagonia to Australia
Homespun Tapestry
Forty Green (Pocket Places)
Who Was She? (Pocket People)
Dear Dad (Pocket People)
Surviving Domestic Violence (Pocket Polemics)

Brenda Eldridge
Connecting

Connecting
ISBN 978 1 76041 741 3
Copyright © text Brenda Eldridge 2019
Celtic knot: Clker-Free-Vector-Images from Pixabay
Cover photos © Stephen Matthews

First published 2019 by
Ginninderra Press
PO Box 3461 Port Adelaide 5015
www.ginninderrapress.com.au

Contents

How Could I Forget	7
More Than Stars	9
Night Magic	10
Destiny	11
No man is an island	12
Next Generations	13
Coming Back	15
Snail	16
An Aerial View	17
When I Stand…	18
Gentle Spring	19
Lilies and Tulips	20
Amsterdam Surprise	21
Windmills	22
Bicycles	23
Tourists	24
Too Fast	26
Sifting Sand	27
What Grace is This?	28
Straight and True	29
Falling Short	30
Pre-dawn	32
Ballachulish	33
Reunion	34
Family Affair	35
Mountaineering	36
Round the World and Back Again	38
Little Gems	39
Earrings Tell a Story	40
Golden Lights	41

Embraced by Sky	43
Dangerous Business	44
What it Means	45
Adult and Child	46
Music in our hearts	48
Transported	49
Wind Like Birds Wings	50
Gulls	51
Fish and Chips	52
Myths and Legends	55
Getting on in age	57
Ruins Under the Sun	58
Tea Time	60
Summer Garden	61
Dying Summer	62
Walking to the Sun	63
Winter Beach	64
Exhilaration	65
Simplicity	67
Will ye no'…	68
Inner Universe	69

How Could I Forget

I hadn't forgotten the clean freshness
Of early morning spring
With dewdrops on fragile grasses
New leaf buds on naked winter trees
Pink and white blossom shyly appearing

But I had forgotten
The pure clarity of songbirds
Hearts bursting with passion
Once so familiar
Not seen or heard for many years

And my favourites –
Wild flowers
Celandines   bluebells   primroses
Growing free in woodlands
At the feet of old castles
For miles beside railway tracks
Transporting me back in time and place
A child again picking a posy
For Mother's Day
Knowing they would wilt so quickly indoors

I sit in my quiet Australian garden
Remembering
So much

More Than Stars

Stars twinkled and shone
Looking like flowers
Close enough to reach up and touch

I watched them for hours
From a train window
Felt they were watching me
Crossing from one side
Of Australia to the other

I learned that Aboriginal people
Don't look at the stars
Rather at the spaces between

Night Magic

The tidal reach
At night
Is black

On the still surface
Stars reflect as
Pinpoints of light

Raindrops falling
Splatter silver exuberance
Energy   movement

Destiny

Gentle rhythm
Water lapping sand
Sunlight flashing
Sparkling in white lace
Gone in a moment
Lingering only in my memory

No two waves alike
Each following its destiny

I am as the waves
Gently following
My destiny

No man is an island

I read of a woman who
In her quest to reach Enlightenment
Lived for twelve years
Alone in a cave in the Himalayas

She made me look again at my own life
Lived with passion in every way
A spiritual richness   a mental maturity
I don't believe I could have achieved
If not for the intimacy with others
The fulfilment of having sons
'For love   pain   and the whole damned thing'

It has been said that no man is an island
Yet even as I longed for the solitude of the cave
I knew to experience life to the fullest
I needed to share it with another
To be sure it was not self-delusion

Next Generations

Pioneers are a particular brand of people
Who grasp opportunities
Forge a new way in an unknown world

Not for them the luxury
Of looking over their shoulder
Lamenting what was left behind

Focus on what's ahead must be maintained
Carrying the casualties
In aching arms and broken hearts

Small wonder then the next generation
Have different needs
Not seduced by the call
Of a wandering star
Preferring to weather life's storms
Within a safe haven
Leaving it to the next generation
To fly like meteors
Through the heavens

Coming Back

Tomorrow I leave
The shores of this
Sunburnt country
(But I am coming back)

This morning the air
Is clearer than ever before
The sense of vastness
Embraces me – it did
From the very beginning
Fifty years ago

Here I have stretched
My mind
My spirit
Never reaching the edges

Snail

I didn't ever doubt it
How like a snail I am
Carrying my home with me
Wherever I go in the world

That doesn't change the warm glow
When I feel it strongly again
A tingle linking me to the earth:
On top of a mountain in Wales
Heart of a beechwood in England
Wildness of Scotland
Remoteness of Kakadu
Vastness of the Red Centre
Rainforests of Tasmania

An Aerial View

My spirit flew like a bird
While my eyes looked down
At the passing world
From on high it was stranger than
Imagination could conjure

The small screen on the seat in front
Told me those lights shining bright far below
Were mystical Sri Lanka

Enormous billowing clouds
Dogged our path to Doha
Was it desert sands that coloured them brown
As they were lit up by cream lightning?
Rising sun a ball of orange fire

Mountains black
Patterned with multi-fingered snow starfish
Stark against a pristine pale blue sky

Seemingly endless miles of red earth
Hours it took to cross Australia
At last a gleam of deep blue ocean over the Bight
Becoming aqua as it lapped against
White beaches
Seeing again familiar places
Excitement building

Full circle I came
From home   to home   to home

When I Stand…

Ocean is everywhere
An unbroken lifeline
Its colours change
As does its temperature
Different areas are home
To a vast array of creatures…

When I stand in the shallows
At the waterline
Here in South Australia
I am standing in
Lochs in Scotland
The Zambezi   Orinoco
Amazon   Ganges   Thames…

And yes! I am connected
To the salmon journeying to spawn
In the same river where they started life
And in turn to the bears
Who stand in the river
Catching the salmon while they are vulnerable
There are birds too
Waiting to help the bears…

This dance of life is
Ever expanding

Gentle Spring

When flowers bloom wherever they can
Brilliant patches of colour
A drift of perfume
Delicate yet so hardy
All too soon comes summer's blaze
Shy blooms close up and sleep
'Perchance to dream'
Until another spring calls them

Lilies and Tulips

Secluded stream
Trickling   sparkling
Hurrying down the mountainside
Pausing in a tree-covered glade
All shades of green
Mixture of north and south hemisphere
In the botanical gardens of Mount Lofty

Here she grew
Tall-stemmed   regal
Among large succulent dark green
Heart-shaped leaves
Not pure white like her arum sister
Green and white lily
Aptly named Green Goddess

I met her distant cousin
Seen in an earthenware pot
On a doorstep in a Netherlands town

Not a lily – a parrot tulip
With exactly the same
Green and white petals
Frilled edges   open   entangled
Not the simple candle-flame shape I knew

Amsterdam Surprise

She stood at the barrier watchful   alert
Huge smiles   tears   hugs
Father and daughter together again

Practicalities of getting cash from a machine

Another beloved voice
'Hello, Grandad'

Surprise rendered us speechless – briefly
Two hours earlier
This one had flown in from Canada
To spend a precious few days
With her family

Windmills

I didn't know the Netherlands
Are as flat as Australia – if not as big
With endless dykes forming
Straight intersecting canals
In towns and countryside alike
Rows of trees acting as windbreaks
Easing the monotony

Windmills   old and new   turned by constant wind
Pumping water back into the rivers
Dykes checked carefully
As they dry out with climate change

What happened to all this
When invasion tanks rumbled through sleepy villages
Their presence still felt in the evening quiet
History so different to ours

Bicycles

Several times a week
I love to ride my bike to the beach
Regardless of the weather

In the Netherlands bikes are serious business

Not for them the fashion statements we have here
Motorist snapping and snarling at us –
Often with good reason

People of all ages proudly ride
Grandparents' 'sit up and beg' style –
Everywhere

Bikes have right of way over –
Everyone
Cars and pedestrians alike

These bikes are custom-made to serve
As carriers of children   pets   furniture
Reminding me of motorbikes seen in Bangkok
So laden it was a wonder they stayed upright

Tourists

We walked cobbled streets
Old towns steeped in history
Marvelling at steel-nerved motorists
Parking cars inches from canal edges

Warmed by vendors
Who immediately spoke English
When they realised we didn't speak Dutch
Never making us feel an imposition

The best times when
Not tourists
We were simply a family together
Sharing meals in unlikely
But interesting places
The sweetest being dinner at home
Around the dining table
So much talking   laughter   love

Too Fast

We were driven to the station
By Stephen's family
Hearts aching for the separation coming
A mellow full moon watched
As if to soften the pain

A train hurtled us from
Rotterdam to Brussels
There panic at another separation – thankfully brief
As my hand slipped from Stephen's
Amid the hordes of pre-Easter travellers
We went through officious
Border controls for the Eurostar to London
Crossing a small corner of Europe
Speed making nonsense of distance
Places I had only been to in books or movies

I felt tension building
As we came out of the Chunnel
Tears flowed

Outside the window was England
My childhood home
My childhood family
Too recently bereft of our mother

Shuddering I stumbled between train stations
Fleeting moments spent
Contemplating taking a different train
Going back to where my life started

But there would be no one there…

Sifting Sand

If each grain of sand
Is a moment in time
How can I measure
My life   any life

Sifting sand
Through my fingers
Are they moments lost

Let the wind
Blow the sand
The moments in time
Into new shapes
Smoothing sharp edges
Of anger and grief
To reveal pristine
Peace

What Grace is This?

Life – so sweet
We cling to you
With such tenacity
Filling our senses
With the magic
Of colour   light   sound

The perfection in a flower
Or a newborn baby's fingernails
Snow-covered mountains
At the dawn of a new day
And in the night sky
Stars paving the way to eternity

Yet at the end
We must leave it all

What Grace is this
That leads us gently away
Taking us fearlessly
Through a gateway
To something beyond
Our knowing?

Straight and True

In *The Prophet**
We are told our children are not our children
As parents we are the bows
From which our children
As living arrows are sent forth
Life's longing for itself

The Archer guides parents
To ensure
The arrows go swift and far

I say to my parents
'You were the bow
And I the arrow
Who went straight   brave   true
Into my own future
Creating a life beyond your imagination

And as a bow myself
I know my children
Have also travelled
Straight   brave   true
And become bows themselves
And their arrows become bows

Do you watch from somewhere
See and are proud
Of your handiwork?'

* *The Prophet* by Kahlil Gibran

Falling Short

I am no longer someone's child
I am free to relish
The knowledge and wisdom
That is mine
From a life well lived

So much we did not share
And in the not telling
Denied ourselves
Knowledge of who we were

But who really knows their parents?
Children watch   listen   learn
And work out for themselves
When the words don't match
The actions

Echoes of
'Don't do as I do   Do as I say'
Don't count for much
Though perhaps they are
Some kind of solace
When tiredness and basic
Human frailty make us fall short
Of what we would really like to do or be

Pre-dawn

Stillness reigns supreme
Over the pre-dawn tidal reach
Fading blue-pink sky
Covers the water
Like a satin sheet
Without wrinkle or crease
Mangrove fringe darkly lush
Air shiver-cool
Fresh on bare skin

Gulls and magpies have acknowledged
A new day approaching
Now silently await the sun

A pelican comes in – flying low
Wingtips almost touching the surface
Meets its perfectly mirrored self
In a splash of bubbles
A ruffle of feathers
Then glides – epitome of grace
Sending ripples slowly to the shores

Once again stillness reigns supreme

Ballachulish

Early morning
Outside our hotel window
Mountains swathed in mist

A yacht moored on the loch
Mast arrow straight
Not a ripple marred its
Reflection on the water

We strolled in cold still air
Sun a brilliant yellow-white glow
Grasses diamond-filled
Bushes of yellow gorse
Delicate larch wearing new spring finery

Threaded through the stillness
Songbirds trilled
Purity reaching far
From such tiny bodies

Reunion

I sat anxiously in the hotel foyer
He strode in
I ran into his arms

He whispered 'I don't do emotions'
I answered 'I do   I cry' and did
His arms tightened

He may not have cried while with us
But he talked   and talked   and talked

Twenty-three years between hugs

Our hungers matched

Family Affair

My brother's arms enfolded me
An embrace that answered all the hungers
Of almost fifty years
Away from my family
The country of my birth

Weeks have gone by and still I have shunned
Reliving those moments with him
Too hard to enjoy them again
Too hard to count the few hours
Harder yet to leave him again

Only this morning I realised
In his arms were Mum and Dad
Our two other brothers
He held me for all of them
And himself

And I, the black sheep of the family
Am banished no longer
I am back in the fold
Which is strange
For I still live
On the other side of the planet

Mountaineering

I gazed in awe at the
West Highlands of Scotland
Knowing my brother has climbed
So many of their peaks
His passion and obsession clear
When he showed them to me
He made me want to climb them too

I am not diminished in the knowledge
I could not do what he does

I reflect on the inner mountains
I have scaled over the same years
Encountering unexpected challenges
Knowing I had only myself to depend on
That preparation is everything –
And even then you can come unstuck

I was asked today
Which one of our parents
Did we get our questing spirit from
And I could not answer

I do know when we reach the heights
We both look around in our solitude
And wonder at the beauty
Only experienced because we put in the effort
And notice the mountains in the distance
Just waiting for us…

Round the World and Back Again

Thirty years ago when my son died
Mother sent me a ring to wear
Rose   yellow   white   gold strands
Twisted like grasses
I never took it off
It held the three of us together

Last year
Her sight gone for long years
Diminished hearing making phone calls impossible
I sent her the ring
Hoping   wearing it   missing me
She would feel it
Remember

When she died earlier this year
The little ring came back to me
Still connecting three generations

Little Gems

A miniature garden
Sits on a cupboard in my studio
It holds symbols
Of a long life
In the corner a gem tree
Leaves of rose quartz
Like spring blossoms

In Inverness we found
Amber gem trees of all sizes
Made in Poland
A little one chose me
Leaves from lemon to burnt umber
Autumn splendour

Earrings Tell a Story

I lost a precious opal earring
It is still hiding in the garden
There can be no replacing it

But I now have amber studs
Myths are many about their tear shape
I wear mine for protection
I hope my fighting days are over

Silver circles holding blue waves
From the west coast of Scotland
They could be dolphins
So like the ones who live
In our tidal reach

Celtic crosses   oval-shaped
Reminding me of the owl of Athena
I always wear on a gold chain

Golden Lights

Coming down a dawn-lit mountain
Trees swayed   tossed
In subdued light
I came round a bend and stopped
To watch in awe as leaves
Had become a mass of gold sparkles
Gently moving like sunlight on the sea
Or was it sprites playing?

Embraced by Sky

Mountains soared
Embraced by bluest sky   billowing clouds
Lower slopes covered in brown grasses
Legendary gold and purple heather
Nothing more than bare grey twigs
Among rocks and crevices
This early in the year

The heights covered in residual snow
Hidden rugged glens always disappearing
Over the next rise
Waterfalls cascading
Cold spray flying high

Lochs mirror still
Reflecting beauty and majesty
Beyond mere words

Dangerous Business

When asked if he had climbed Ben Nevis
He said, 'Only the easy way
The other way climbers need to be roped together'

Climbing with his sons
He was too aware of danger
Said he wouldn't want to live with the consequences
If one of them fell…

When I was a young mother raising sons
I didn't know
We were climbing mountains too
Never imagined the weakest
In our family would cause one to fall

I spent far too many years
Being afraid of the weakest link
Believing it was me
Who had failed our boys

He too is dead now
We who are left are strong
But climbing our individual mountains
Made us insular

What it Means

A man was asked
What it means to have a son
He said
It was the end of his youth

As a mother I knew this to be a truth
Seeing more clearly
How my own sons have changed
As they held newborn sons
In their arms
Watched as those children took
Their first steps
Knowing they were the
First of many
That would take them away
Yet encouraging them to succeed

How does a man feel
When his sons are grown men
With children of their own

Can he quietly celebrate
That he overcame the desire
To hold them back
Keep them dependent on him
Be proud that they are
Better men than himself

Adult and Child

The adult me pretended
I was cool about riding
The Jacobite train from
Fort William to Mallaig
Purchasing a gift for a grandson on the train
The poet and artist silenced
Awed by the grandeur of Glenfinnan viaduct
The majesty of mountains

The child in me was so excited!
I was riding on the Hogwarts Express
And there was NOTHING
That could spoil the magic of that!

I bought the Harry Potter wand
But secretly lusted for one of my own –
A real one I could use
To change the world into a better place

Music in our hearts

Several times we saw them
Lone pipers on a busy street
Kilts swaying to an inner beat
Hypnotic   beautiful   when heard outside
Tugging at unknown places within
Making tears sting our eyes
Our mouths tremble

On our tour bus
We were privileged to hear
Traditional Gaelic music
Played through a smart phone
By our musician/driver from Skye

Amid the towering mountains
Blue lochs   flickering sunlight
We were all –
From Australia   America   England alike
Rendered silent
Transported by a heartbreaking lament
Needing no words

Transported

I listen to lilting notes
Of a favourite piano piece
That gifts me calm
For all the movement of sound

I look out of the window
Clouds drift across the
Early evening sky
Sun visibly sinking
Even as it highlights
The tidal reach with sparkles
Dancing like the music

Leaves are moving in a gentle breeze
Shivering as the plants
Are anchored in the earth

My heart beats steadily
My senses are moved by
Sound   light   movement
As I sit here in the stillness

Wind Like Birds Wings

I put breadcrumbs out on the path
Sparrows come down
Hovering briefly before they land
Turning the garden into
A flutter of movement
Much like wind through leaves
Flickering   rustling
Bending flower stems
Making shadows of trees dance
On the sitting room floor

Gulls

I watch in admiration
As our silver gulls soar on a gusty wind
Swoop intrepidly to snatch food
From an unsuspecting hand
But they have no plaintive voices
Only sullen raucous squawking

I was filled with anticipation
To hear the distinctive calls
Of the herring gulls

I wasn't disappointed

We sat on a harbour wall
Eating highly recommended
And fabulous fish and chips
Among lobster pots and coils of rope
Watching fishing boats and ferries
Timeless activities

Three gulls joined us
They were huge!
Accepting with beautiful manners
Our offerings – no fighting or squabbling

Lunch finished
Our gull friends flew off
Leaving their haunting cries on the wind

Fish and Chips

Living far inland
(If tiny England can have far)
Fresh fish was a luxury for us as children
Things inevitably changed with time
In my teens
Fish and chips became a new treat

Years later
Fish and chips are still a treat
As takeaway from our local man
To be enjoyed at home
On our balcony
Overlooking the tidal reach
Greedy gulls always hovering too close

Whenever we visit Tasmania
We go to Hobart wharf
Sipping sparkling wine
Trying not to burn our mouths
On vinegar-drenched lunch
Moored yachts and Antarctic explorers
Fascinating company
Mount Wellington an ever-brooding presence

For all its fancy cuisine
Elegant tableware
We preferred cod and chips
In a quiet Inverness pub
Next door to our hotel
Beside the river Ness

But when all is said and done
Homemade crumbed whiting – à la Stephen –
Served with rosemary and salt chips
And peas
Cannot be beaten anywhere

Myths and Legends

Just after the war
My parents moved into an old farmhouse
Mother said when she was alone
She heard whistling
As if someone were coming round the path

I didn't hear the whistling
I felt the presence
Of a Roman soldier lingering
In the stairwell
He was gone when I visited over thirty years ago –
He didn't like my gift of windchimes
Perhaps one hundred tiny brass bells was too much
Or too exotic for that most English of houses

The bunyip appears
In Aboriginal mythology
Living in billabongs or waterways
Tales about it leave
An unsettling feeling
An unanswered 'What if…'

The small cruise boat
Eased out into Loch Ness
Beneath an eerily clouded sky
Water grey uninviting
White wash followed us
Folding in on itself
Our scepticism alive and well
As the guide told us
One of many stories that abound

What was it then
That caused the water to ripple
In the distance?
No other vessel in sight
Barely any wind…

Getting on in age

Over the years we have seen a parade
Of people walking along the river-path
Mostly with a dog or two
We have seen the injured getting better
Elderly and ill getting more and more frail
Disorientated troubled souls
Disappear with no warning
Some have said hello in passing
Others not a word of acknowledgement

An elderly couple in our group
Had been travelling for weeks
He was weary of it all
Longed to go home
Mind befuddled he sat on the trains
Passing through magnificent scenery
Head down doing a crossword

She often lingered talking to others
Needing company
Whistling to him if he strayed too far

We watched boats coming down
The flight of locks that are Neptune's Staircase
A miracle of engineering

She whistled
To get his attention
But only a sheepdog came running

Black humour

Ruins Under the Sun

Countless ruins crouch on stony paddocks
Mile after mile of rolling emptiness
Old trees still shading broken walls
Testament to stalwart tenacity
Migrants seeking to build a new life
Far from familiar shores
War monuments in small country towns
Telling the tragic story of men gone forever

We passed ruinous crofters cottages
Desolation amid the grandeur
A stone wall   a chimney stack
Telling another tale of stark rawness
Life a struggle against weather
Poor soil   greed of landowners

I have heard the lamenting
Of women and children on the wind
Keening for their menfolk
Who will never come home again
Wives for husbands
Mothers for sons
Sisters for brothers
Daughters for fathers

Lives shattered
Grief as unrelenting
As the changing seasons

Teatime

Make a pot of tea
Using loose leaves
None of those tea bags
Pause to let it brew
Then pour
Into a dainty cup with saucer

What is it about the smell
That can transport me in an instant
Back to cups of tea
Drunk in the old farm garden

A summer thing
Surrounded by the smell of
Newly mown grass
The gentle hum of bees
Busy in the flowers

Timeless teatime

Summer Garden

Petunias become emblems
Of a summer garden
Eye-catching in their pots
Seeming to need little water
Thriving on neglect
In return their sweet scent
Fills the still air
And I rejoice in their flamboyance

Dying Summer

Smell of hay and straw fills my senses
As I walk across the dunes
The very essence of dying summer

Dry sand cold as it sifts
Into my sandals
Settles between my toes

Sea exquisite silver blue
Waterline a melody of percussion sounds
Shushing   glopping   hissing

Low sun casting long long shadows

Mine this beautiful morning
Gift of another day

Walking to the Sun

I wade westwards
Loving the feel of the cold sea
Sloshing around my legs
Only little wavelets
Constant movement

Then it's time to go time
And I turn and walk back to shore
Aware of the play of sunbeams
Through water
Lozenges of light
On the surface

I am walking to the sun
But it is what I have always done

Winter Beach

Sea mist obscuring the horizon
Makes container ships look like
They are floating in mid-air
Not on the water

Sea dull fog-grey
Wide expanse of sand
All waiting and watching patiently
As the sun breaks through
Thinning cloud
Creating blue patches of eternity

Small fishing vessel
Racing down the gulf
Leaving a white wake

Long long waves coming in singly
Gently heaving over
A curl of dark grey
Edged by white froth

A pair of gulls
Bobbing together in a ritual dance

Not another person in sight

In this stillness
My heart and mind
Settle to the rhythm of the ocean

Exhilaration

If a day needed a word
This day was
Exhilaration

Heavy clouds were scudding across the sky
Leaving patches of pristine blue
Allowing shafts of sunlight to escape
Dispelling all gloom

As I crossed the bridge
There came a sudden squall
Wind too strong for me to continue cycling
Icy rain blown sideways
Stabbing against my head and face

The sea was rough
Rolling in full of energy
Wonderful around my legs
While laughter flew with the spray

Back on the path
Not properly balanced
Another gust of wind
Sent me and my bike to the rocks

Grazed knees a reminder all day
Of the exhilaration I felt

Simplicity

A single drop of water
Hanging from a leaf
Sparkles with rainbow colours

No need for a fanfare
All is held in silence
By sunlight

Will ye no'…

Rain on the teeth of a biting wind
I had looked for in the Scottish Highlands
Instead balmy spring days
Swaths of wild flowers
Songbirds – hearts bursting with joy and lust

Here on this Australian shore
Westerly winds tear at hair   coat
Making me shiver
As low dark grey clouds
Race across hidden blue
Bringing longed-for drought-breaking rain

And another drought broken
Long long years between hugs
But the words of a song
Flicker through my mind
'Will ye no' come back again?'

Inner Universe

A poet wrote of seeing the world in a grain of sand
And eternity in an hour
But I was unable to grasp the real meaning
Though I liked the sound of it

I have dared myself to look upward
Into the vast night sky and ponder
Something that has no end
No safe edges
And learned not to be afraid

I like to see patches of blue
Between billowing clouds
They are a glimpse of eternity

Where did this certainty come from
That the universe was inside me?
Another gift of faith that mere words
Cannot define

Once again it is the finite mind
Trying to embrace the infinite
And for this there can only be
Surrender to acceptance

www.ingramcontent.com/pod-product-compliance
Lightning Source LLC
Chambersburg PA
CBHW062154100526
44589CB00014B/1835